POCKET IMAGES

Pembrokeshire Returns

Group of three Llangwm fisherwomen photographed by Seth Griffiths in 1912.

POCKET IMAGES

Pembrokeshire
Returns

D. Ken Daniels

NONSUCH

Acknowledgements

I wish to record with grateful thanks the generous assistance given to me by many people during the preparation of this book. They include:

Lord Gordon Parry of Neyland; Mrs Lily Cordon; Mr Albert Howells; Mrs Anne Morris; Mr Phil Harris; Mr Gwyn Briwnant Jones; the staff of Tenby Library; Mrs Nancy Davies; Mr Cedric Morgan; Mrs Joyce Lewis; Mr Winston Jones; Miss Emily Edwards; Mr Roscoe Howells; Simon Eckley (Wales editor of Chalford Publishing).

First published 1996
This new pocket edition 2006
Images unchanged from first edition

Nonsuch Publishing Limited
The Mill, Brimscombe Port,
Stroud, Gloucestershire, GL5 2QG
www.nonsuch-publishing.com

Nonsuch Publishing is an imprint of Tempus Publishing Group

British Library Cataloguing in Publication Data.
A catalogue record for this book is available from the British Library.

ISBN 1-84588-305-5

Typesetting and origination by Nonsuch Publishing Limited
Printed in Great Britain by Oaklands Book Services Limited

St Thomas Reading Room A.F.C., Prendergast, Haverfordwest, 1909. Photograph by Seth Griffiths.

Contents

Foreword

by Gordon Parry

The very young tend to be scathing about nostalgia. That's understandable. Their 'past' lies in the future. For those of us who, to say the least, are not very young, nostalgia, memorabilia and ephemera sustain our memories and keep us in touch with all those things in our lives that we have no wish to forget. Young people probably understand home-sickness better. It might well be within their own shorter experience of life. They might already have felt that *hiraeth* - that longing for contact with home and friends that overtakes almost everyone at some time or another in lonely moments.

Having known Ken Daniels since he was barely out of his teens, and Lucille, his wife, for just as long a time - we were colleagues from its opening day in 1952 at the 'New School' (now the Sir Thomas Picton School) in Haverfordwest - I have no difficulty in seeing him as he was on his first weekend out of Pembrokeshire, about to commence college studies, a stranger in a foreign land called London.

In a sense, we owe this book and its forerunner - the immensely popular *Saundersfoot and Tenby*, published in the Archive Photographs Series by Chalford in time for it to become Pembrokeshire's best selling book of the summer - to the young Ken's friendly landlady. She suggested that he visit the local market to pass an hour. At the perfect moment for him, when loneliness and inevitable home-sickness were threatening, he discovered postcard pictures of his lately-left Saundersfoot in a box full of bargains.

Since then Ken has become one of Britain's foremost collectors of postcards and an expert on antiques and ephemera of every kind. Lucille has happily shared his enthusiasms. Very recently, at my home, my wife and I shared the better part of a day with the Daniels. While we reminisced about various people and occasions during the last forty years of our friendship, Ken and I had met for a purpose. It was for him to take me through the material already collated for *Pembrokeshire Returns*. I found each postcard fascinating and the nostalgic tour of our home county on which its author took me, without either of us leaving our seats, a joy.

From the beaches and mountains of Mynydd Preseli, in the north, to our own 'down below' green farmlands, county villages and small towns, I was taken back into my childhood and the history of my county, long before my birth here more than seventy years ago.

Even better, as a former Chairman of the Wales Tourist Board, I knew that, nationally and internationally, the new collection would capture or recall for our visitors, something of the magic that was Wales. Then, when they come to see Wales for themselves, they will discover what a vibrant, modern country ours has become. Nostalgia doesn't trap you in the past. It teaches tradition and history, inspires pride in your origins and the people who created your culture and gives you the foundation on which the future is built.

Gordon Parry.

Brigadier Chaplain Major, Revd Ceitho Davies addresses the troops from a boxing ring at Penally Camp, 1922.

Introduction

It was during 1974 that Pembrokeshire as a county disappeared in the reorganisation of local government. The three counties of Pembrokeshire, Carmarthen and Cardigan were re-designated as the Dyfed authority with its administrative headquarters at Carmarthen.

As from 1 April 1996, the county reverts back to its former status. Many people of Pembrokeshire (*Sir Benfro*) will wholeheartedly welcome and proclaim this return. The publication of this pictorial book therefore coincides with, and celebrates, the reappearance of Pembrokeshire.

We have been most fortunate with Pembrokeshire's Edwardian photographers who had various photographic studios in different parts of the county. Besides their portrait studies, they left a fascinating pictorial legacy of postcards. This great historical resource includes topographical town and village scenes and many views of great events, forgotten patterns of work and colourful local characters. Many such splendid images were originally available for purchase from these photographer's respective studios.

During the 'Golden Age of Postcards' the following productive photographic studios were to be found in Pembrokeshire:

> Charles Edwards, Main Street, Fishguard;
> S. G. (Seth) Griffiths, Haverfordwest;
> David Bowen, Caer Alun, Picton Place, Haverfordwest;
> S. J. (Sam) Allen, Bush Street, Pembroke Dock;
> H. Mortimer Allen, Excelsior, High Street, Tenby;
> Arthur Squibbs, Warren Street, Tenby;
> William G. Morris, The Chemist, Saundersfoot.
> Willie John, Clunderwen.

Besides the local photographers, there were many national producers of Pembrokeshire postcards including such well known publishers as Raphael Tuck, Francis Frith, Valentine, Wrench, and Judges.

The fascination with the distant past in pictures is never-ending. Our yearning for nostalgia appears undiminished especially when we look back at our friendly and close-knit communities of Pembrokeshire. For the younger generation, the opportunity to learn of its historical background and the social and economic circumstances of the past should influence their opinion on Pembrokeshire's future.

Finally, allow me to re-iterate that my aim and pleasure in producing this book is to welcome the return of our lovely county of Pembrokeshire and to congratulate all those who have worked hard to achieve this end.

D. Ken Daniels
Saundersfoot.

General view of the Lower Fishguard harbour from Penslade, 1904. The herring trawlers (drifters) and coastal trading vessels then brought prosperity to the community. Photograph by Charles Edwards.

One

Fishguard (*Abergwaun*) and Goodwick (*Wdig*)

High Street leading from the main square in Fishguard with a donkey waiting patiently for its master, c. 1905. Many businesses and public houses flourished in the area at this time.

High Street, Fishguard, leading south of the main square, 1906.

The Great Western Hotel and Cornock the hairdresser, High Street, Fishguard, 1907. The hotel was established before the arrival of the town's railway. There were daily connections to and from the Haverfordwest GWR station.

Market Square, Fishguard with the Commercial Inn and St Mary's Church on the right, 1922.

Locals and the duty policeman pose on Fishguard Square for photographer, Charles Edwards, 1911.

11

Lower Fishguard showing the road bridge over the River Gwaun, 1908. The picturesque Gwaun valley cuts inland, top right.

Inside the power station at Fishguard, c. 1910. Situated at the northern end of the port, it supplied electricity to the locality.

Fishguard Harbour GWR station nearing completion, 1905. Photograph by Charles Edwards.

"Mauretania Special" Fishguard Station.

The signal is down and the first 'Mauretania Special' is about to leave for London from Fishguard station, 14.52, 30 August 1909. The train on this occasion was headed by engines No 3402 (Halifax) and No 4108 (Gardenia).

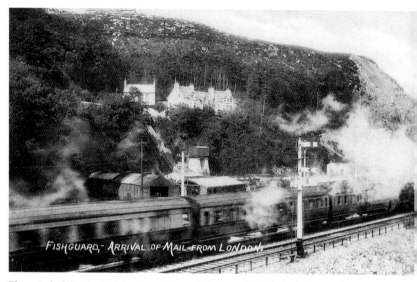

The arrival of the Royal Mail train at Fishguard Harbour, 1910. In the background is the Fishguard Bay Railway Hotel.

Three steamers being unloaded by harbour cranes, 1907. The importance to Fishguard of the Irish cattle trade through the port is well illustrated by the large number of cattle pens, lairages and trucks. Photograph by Charles Edwards.

MAURETANIA IN FISHGUARD HARBOUR AUGUST 30TH 1909. PHOTO GRIFFITHS.

The *Mauretania* at anchor for the first time in Fishguard Harbour, 30 August 1909. To mark this special occasion all the schoolchildren of the district were presented with a commemorative mug and large crowds gathered in wonderment to watch the arrival of this gigantic Cunard liner. Photograph by Seth Griffiths.

Passengers' luggage is loaded onto the SS *Great Western* tender, 1909. The other two tenders, SS *Sir Francis Drake* and SS *Smeaton*, were responsible for the transport of the passengers and mailbags respectively. Photograph by Charles Edwards.

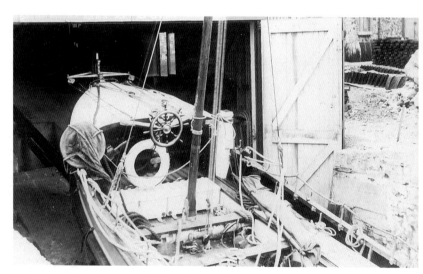

TRAIN SERVICES from FISHGUARD

Connecting with the Cork/Fishguard
DIRECT EXPRESS PASSENGER SERVICE
"THE INNISFALLEN WAY."

Steamer leaves Cork (Penrose Quay) at 6.8 p.m., for Fishguard Harbour Mondays, Wednesdays and Fridays.

Steamer arrives Fishguard Harbour about 3 a.m. Tuesdays, Thursdays and Saturdays.

STATION		Trains Depart.		
	a.m.	a.m.	a.m.	a.m.
FISHGUARD Harb. dep.	3.55	4N55	8.15	
Swansea (High Street) arr.	5.33	6N37	10.52	
Cardiff (General) ...	6.35	7N53	12.4	
Newport	7.1	8N16	12.26	
Hereford	9.0	9.51	2Z10	
Shrewsbury ...	11.10	11F30	3Z20	
Worcester (Foregate Street)	—	10.43	3.24	
Birmingham (Snow Hill) ...	—	11.46	4.30	
Bristol (Stapleton Road)	8.2	9N9	1.19	
Bristol (Temple Meads)	8.14	9N18	1W35	
Bath	8.55	9N45	1.43	
Salisbury ...		12d35	3.8	
Southampton (Central)	11K26	1P22	3U51	
Portsmouth and Southsea	12M30	2Q0	4U42	
Weymouth ...	11.42	11N42	4.8	
Taunton ...	9.47	11.30	2W36	
Exeter (St. David's) ...	10.37	12.13	3W20	
Plymouth (North Road)	12.25	1e55	4W52	
Gloucester	8.42	10G18	3.31	
Cheltenham Spa (St. James)	9.41	10Y32	4.20	
Oxford	10K9	11.54	5R25	
Reading	9.0	10.45	3.25	
Farnborough (North) ...	10.28	11.44	4.58	
Aldershot	10.46	12.2	5.15	
LONDON (Paddington) ...	9.45	10N45	3.10	

Q—Via Reading. On Sats. until Sept. 14th (inc.) arr. 12.49 p.m., and on Sept. 21st and 28th, to 1.19 p.m. R—On Sats. until Sept. 7th (inc.) arr. 4.35 p.m. via Reading. U—Via Salisbury. V—On Sats. dep. 4.20 p.m. W—On Sats. arr. Bristol 2.7 p.m., Exeter 3.30 p.m. and Plymouth 3.40 p.m. Taunton 3.50 p.m. Y—One class only for portion of journey : Malvern Rd. Sn. St. James arr. 10.51 a.m. On Sats arr. Cheltenham South and Leckhampton 11.16 a.m. or St. James' 12.3 p.m. (1st and 3rd class). Z—On Sats. arr. Hereford 1.59 and Shrewsbury 3.6 p.m. *—These fares also apply from Cork to the Stations named. †—Passengers by the 11.55 a.m. train from Paddington may go on board steamer upon arrival of train at Fishguard. d—On Tues. arr. Salisbury 11.7 a.m. e—On Sats. arr. Plymouth 3.38 p.m. until Sept. 14th and 2.10 p.m. on Sept. 21st and 28th. T—Transfer to Saloon. T—Transfer to Saloon.—Passengers holding First Class Tickets may transfer to Saloon of Steamer on payment on board at Fishguard or in the Office at Cork, as the case may be, of 10/- Single, 15/- Return. Children

Train timetable for connections with the Fishguard to Cork 'direct express passenger service' operated by the 3,250 ton Innisfallen, *July 1935. The ship travelled at an average speed of 18 knots.*

The lifeboat, *Charterhouse* was a gift from the past and present Carthusians. It cost £2,948 and was launched in October 1908. Photograph by Charles Edwards.

Fishguard dignitaries pose for Charles Edwards at the launch of the lifeboat, *Charterhouse*.

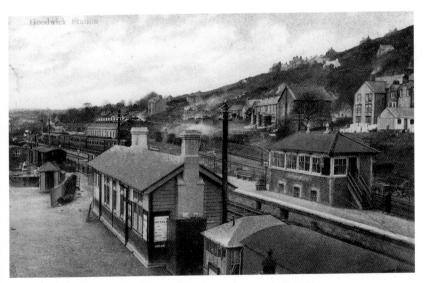

Goodwick GWR station showing the signal box and engine sheds, 1908.

Above: Main Street, Goodwick, 1911.

Left: Mr Miles' refreshment rooms, Goodwick, 1909.

Above: Religious meeting at Fishguard Top, 1905. Many such meetings were held in Pembrokeshire and elsewhere in West and South Wales during a religious revival inspired by the charismatic leadership of Evan Roberts. The region was swept by mass outpourings of non-conformist spiritual fervour and many a chapel owes its construction or extension due to the increase in the congregations at this time. Photograph by Charles Edwards.

Right: Ben Jones of Fishguard, the Welsh amateur lightweight boxing champion. He won his title on 24 February 1912 at the age of twenty-one. He was guided and trained by the well-known Tom Furlong (right).

BEN·JONES·FISHGUARD.
AMATUER·LIGHTWEIGHT·CHAMPION·OF·WALES.
AND·HIS·TRAINER·T·H·FURLONG.

Shemi Wad, Fishguard and Goodwick's famous story-teller (*cyfarwydd*), 1904. Many tall and colourful tales were told by this local character. Photograph by Charles Edwards.

ONE OF THE OLD BRIGADE.

Pub by D. L. Llewellyn, Goodwick.

Jim Herrington, an Irish tramp who travelled the roads of North Pembrokeshire. This 'king of the road' was a veteran of the Crimean War who, at the age of seventy-five, was found dead in an out building of Fishguard's Royal Oak Inn on 5 September 1906.

Two

Haverfordwest (*Hwlffordd*): The County Town

A lithograph of Castle Square and High Street, Haverfordwest, c. 1850.

A gathering of the rich and important, outside the Shire Hall (right of picture), Victoria Place, Haverfordwest, 1912.

Stephen Green's imposing store-front at the bottom of High Street, Haverfordwest. The message dated 12 June 1912 on the back of the postcard reads: 'Mr Gwyther will be in Letterston Fair next Monday when he hopes to be favoured with your kind orders. If there are any goods which we can send on Monday to meet you there, the matter shall have our best attention. Awaiting your commands.'

Above: A busy High Street in 1909. The businesses seen in the foreground belonged to George Ace of Tenby and David Davies (both on the left of the street) with the premises of Cash & Co. and Rees Bros. on the right.

Right: The imposing and prosperous business of Greenish and Dawkins, Commerce House, Haverfordwest, 1903. This fashion store was then considered as Pembrokeshire's principal place for ladies' outfitting, drapery and millinery.

THE WEST WALES SHOPPING CENTRE.

COMMERCE HOUSE, HAVERFORDWEST.

23

Market Street, Haverfordwest, 1906.

Upper Market Street, Haverfordwest, 1906.

The Pembrokeshire Infirmary at St Thomas Green, Haverfordwest, 1904.

Haverfordwest Grammar School for Boys in Dew Street, c. 1906, with the Fish Market in the background (later the Municipal Milk Dairy).

Mary Tasker's School for Girls, Tower Hill, Haverfordwest, 1908.

Mariners' Square at the Junction of Dark Street and Tower Hill, Haverfordwest, 1910.

Spring Gardens, Haverfordwest, 1908.

Advertisement for George Thomas, a saddler and harness-maker of No 13 Quay Street, Haverfordwest, 1906.

Unloading limestone below the New Bridge in Haverfordwest, 1904. It was taken to Warlow's Bartlett lime kilns.

Panoramic view of Haverfordwest from The Parade, 1904. Photograph by David Bowen.

Salutation Square and Picton Place, Haverfordwest, 1906. Photograph by David Bowen.

A later 1911 view from a slightly different angle giving a more complete view of the Salutation Hotel. It was from this hotel that the presiding judge travelled by police escort to the assizes at the nearby Shire Hall.

Haverfordwest Boy Scouts at Scotchwells, 1909-10. Photograph by David Bowen.

Left: the Pembrokeshire County War Memorial which was unveiled on 3 September 1921 by Mr Hubert Lewis of Milford Haven. Private Lewis had been awarded the Victoria Cross for extreme gallantry while serving in the First World War. *Right*: the programme for the re-dedication ceremony for the County War Memorial which took place on 2 September 1973. The memorial was re-sited next to the Masonic Hall to allow for road improvements associated with the southern by-pass scheme.

The GWR staff and associates make an impressive group for photographer, Seth Griffiths, 1909. Seated is station-master, Mr F. Langford (third from the left in the front row) and standing extreme left is Mr George Bland who held carting contracts to deliver goods from the railway station.

Bridgend Square, Haverfordwest in 1903. Bland's carriage building business is on the left. Photograph by David Bowen.

Llewellin's churnworks, North Gate, Haverfordwest, 1908. Manufacturers of dairy and butter churns, this was one of the oldest and most important businesses in the town. The buildings were demolished in 1987 to make way for a new roundabout.

George Llewellin and his creamery staff at the churnworks in 1910. Photograph by Seth Griffiths.

Official opening of Scotchwells, Haverfordwest, 25 June 1908. Photograph by Seth Griffiths.

Hill Park ladies on a day trip to Broad Haven, c. 1909. The horses and waggonette belonged to George Bland of Bridgend Square. Photograph by David Bowen.

Old Prendergast Paper Mill, Haverfordwest, 1903. Located on a leet from the Western Cleddau river, it had originally been operated as a corn mill. Photograph by David Bowen.

Walter Roach is chaired by his jubilant supporters outside the Mariners' Hotel after his election as Liberal MP in a 1908 by-election. Photograph by Seth Griffiths.

Haverfordwest Agricultural Show on the Bridge Meadow, July 1908. Photograph by Seth Griffiths.

Bridge Street athletic team, 1913. Photograph by Seth Griffiths.

Proclamation of the accession to the throne of King George V, Shire Hall, Haverfordwest, 9 May 1910. Photograph by Seth Griffiths.

Parade of Red Cross nurses on Castle Square in Haverfordwest, 1909. Photograph by Seth Griffiths.

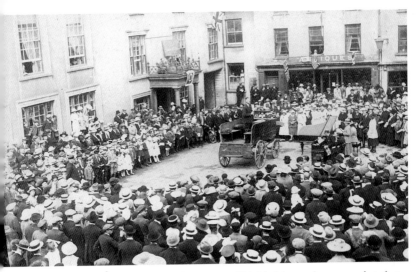

A Suffragette Movement meeting at Castle Square in 1910. Mrs Massey, about to speak, is first being introduced to a large gathering of local people. Photograph by Seth Griffiths.

Lloyd George (just visible above the crowd hands on hips with his back to camera) speaks to a mass of local people in High Street, Haverfordwest, 1922. Photograph by Seth Griffiths.

Left: Entry from supporters of the Suffragette Movement at the Haverfordwest Carnival of July 1909. The float carried the slogans: 'Blokes for Women' and 'We Must Have Votes for Women'. Photograph by David Bowen.

Below: Invitation card for the Mayor's Coronation celebration held at the Market Hall in Haverfordwest on 13 May 1937.

KING GEORGE VI &
QUEEN ELIZABETH

CORONATION
MAY 12TH 1937

PRINTED & MADE IN ENGLAND

Market Hall, Haverfordwest

The Mayor's Coronation Celebration

THURSDAY, MAY 13th, 1937

Whist Championship and Other Prizes.	Dancing 10 p.m. to 3 a.m.

Music by: Teddy Holmes and His Band.

TICKETS · · · · 2/6.

The unveiling ceremony for the South African (Boer) War Memorial below St Mary's Church, Haverfordwest, 21 October 1904. Lord Cawdor, several other local dignitaries and officials and a police band were in attendance.

The Havard brothers pictured during the construction of the wall around the South African War Memorial, High Street, Haverfordwest, c. 1905. Photograph by David Bowen.

Cricket pavilion, the racecourse, Haverfordwest, 11 June 1919. Photograph by Seth Griffiths.

Staff of the Maypole Dairy Co. Ltd, Bridge Street, Haverfordwest, 1926.

Right: Embellished bill, dated 10 April 1885, from James Rees, provision merchant of Bridge Street, Haverfordwest.

Below: Parcel label from James Adams & Son, Haverfordwest, c. 1920.

BRIDGE STREET,

Haverfordwest. Apl 10 1885

Mr Bennett

Bot of James Rees.

TEA, COFFEE, SPICE,

Flour & Provision Merchant.

TERMS – CASH.

5% CENT PER ANNUM CHARGED ON ALL OVERDUE A/cs.

LADIES' HIGH-CLASS TAILORING
A SPECIALITY

James Adams & Son

DRAPERS
AND MILLINERS

MANCHESTER HOUSE, BRIDGE STREET
HAVERFORDWEST   TEL. 194

DATE ....   PER ....

COUNTY THEATRE, HAVERFORDWEST

THURSDAY AFTERNOON;
FEBRUARY 1st, 1945

At 2.30 p.m.

Recital for
MRS. CHURCHILL'S RED CROSS
"AID TO RUSSIA" FUND

MOISEIWITSCH

PROGRAMME

Ballade in F major	....	
Waltz in A flat major	....	CHOPIN
Etude in C major, Op. 10	....	
Sonata in B minor, Op. 58	....	
Two Fairy Tales	....	MEDTNER
Two Preludes	....	RACHMANINOFF
Nocturne for left hand	....	SCRIABIN
Study in F sharp major	....	STRAVINSKY
Pictures from an Exhibition	....	MOUSSORGSKY

Direction: IBBS & TILLETT, LONDON.

TICKETS: 7/6, 5/-, 3/6 (all reserved)
Obtainable at Pembrokeshire Community Council,
Panteg House, Salutation Square,
(Tel. H'West 297) HAVERFORDWEST

This Recital is being held on behalf of the War Organisation of the British Red Cross Society and the Order of St. John of Jerusalem, registered under the War Charities Act, 1940.

VAIL & Co., Ltd., Printers, W.1

Programme for the performance of *Moiseiwitsch* at the County Theatre, Haverfordwest, 1 February 1945.

TASKER'S HIGH SCHOOL
MAGAZINE

How Much Better is it to get
Wisdom than Gold.

1946

EDITOR M. THWAITES.

This, our first post-war magazine is yet another sign of our gradual return to normal conditions and activities. Shortage of paper and our patriotic efforts to do without everything except the essential, have prevented the production of a periodical of this kind during the war years. To the present members of the school this venture is entirely new. Like all first efforts it lacks many things, but, incomplete though it is, I hope it may be an incentive to many of you to become contributors to future issues.

The purpose of such a magazine is to put on record the activities of the school in every field, the "doings" of our Old Girls and interesting facts concerning individuals among them, and to serve as an outlet for the literary aspirations of all our girls from the youngest to the members of Form VI.

This number, I believe, covers all these aims, though in some fields somewhat sparse perhaps. May good luck follow in its train.

In July we shall be losing Miss Calvin Thomas, who has been our Domestic Science Mistress for nearly twenty years. During this long period she has given yeoman service to the school. We shall miss her, not only in the realm of cookery, for she is highly skilled in the culinary art and has done much, through the medium of her pupils, to expel monotony from the war-time menus of many homes, but much more shall we miss her in the general life of the school, where her gentle nature and cultured outlook will leave their stamp for many years to come. May she enjoy a long and happy retirement.

By the time this magazine is published the term will be drawing to a close. Happy holidays to all.

N. M. SMITH.

First post-War magazine at Tasker's High School for Girls, summer term 1946.

42

Above: The newly appointed Chief Constable of Pembrokeshire, Mr Alan Goodson with retired members of the Pembrokeshire Police Force at the Police Headquarters, Haverfordwest, 1965. From left to right, back row: PC 78 J.C. Evans; PC 46 C.L. Richards; Supt and DCC R.J. Jones; PC 53 D. Davies; Chief Inspector R.W. Jones; Mr Alan Goodson Chief Constable; Supt. and DCC W.E. John; Supt M.S. Roberts; Chief Inspector W.I. Morgans; PC 19 J.H. Watts. Middle row: PC 37 S.J. Thomas; Supt and DCC C.B. James; PS 5 L.T. Rees; PS 11 J.H. John; Inspector W.I. Evans; PC 27 B. Williams; PC 79 D.W.E. Mason; PS N. Wilnow; PS F. James; PS 24 J.F. Thomas; Chief Inspector J.R. Savage: PC 29 W.J.C. Wren. Front row: Chief Inspector P. Phillips; PC 76 J.A. Bowen; PS 14 F.W.J. Hughes; Inspector H.G. Hart; PC 51 D. Davies; PC 75 D.S. James; PSI W.J. Wood; PC 34 L.J. Edwards; Supt B. Williams; PC 56 J. Thomas.

Right: Programme from the service of commemoration for 111 years of community service by the Pembrokeshire Police, St David's Cathedral, 17 March 1968.

ST. DAVIDS CATHEDRAL

———

PEMBROKESHIRE POLICE
1857 - 1968

———

A Service of Commemoration

on

SUNDAY, 17th MARCH, 1968

in the presence of
Her Majesty's Lieutenant of the County of Pembroke
(Col. The Honourable Hanning Philipps, M.B.E.)

———

EGLWYS GADEIRIOL TY DDEWI

Procession of a military band and marching soldiers down the High Street in Haverfordwest, c. 1900. James Adams, the draper, watches the proceedings from the doorway of his shop. Later, the business moved to Manchester House, Bridge Street.

Three

Milford Haven
(*Aberdaugleddau*)

Hamilton Terrace, Milford Haven, c. 1900.

Hamilton Terrace, Milford Haven, c. 1900. The buildings shown include Marine Villa, Hamilton House and St Katherine's Church.

Upper Parade, Hamilton Terrace, Milford Haven, 1904. Photograph by Seth Griffiths.

The Lord Nelson Hotel at the lower end of Hamilton Terrace, 1929. An excellent view of the docks and the Haven was available from the hotel. At the bus stop two of Green's buses can be seen en route to Haverfordwest and Neyland.

Parallel to Hamilton Terrace is Charles Street, seen here c. 1912. Many provision merchants and retail stores were based here in Milford Haven's main street.

Above: Charles Street, Milford Haven, 1908.

Left: The John Cory Sailors' Bethel Mission of Rest, Charles Street, Milford Haven, c. 1912. The mission assisted in the welfare of seamen throughout their stay in port.

Dockside at Milford Haven, c. 1905. The Bradbury and Rees coal wagons in the foreground are waiting to fuel the steam trawlers.

A catch being landed during the halcyon days of the fishing industry in Milford Haven, c. 1907.

The daily sale of fish at Milford Haven fishmarket, 1912.

The dockside offices of fish salesmen, Mitchell Brothers and the appropriately named F. Salmon & Son, and the Atlantic Engineering Co, Milford Haven, 1910. Photograph by Seth Griffiths.

The Slip, Milford Haven

Milford Haven trawler No 127 in for repairs at the dry dock slip, 1913.

OPENING THE DOCK GATES, MILFORD HAVEN.

The manually operated dock gates at Milford Haven, c. 1911.

The steel Victoria Bridge linking Milford Haven and Hakin, 1910.

GWR sidings filled with the coal wagons of several companies, c. 1920. The Victoria Bridge is in the background.

Havens Head and Milford Haven GWR station, c. 1912.

The children of upper Hill Street, Hakin, pose for the photographer, 1906.

The Priory ruins with the smoking chimney of the saw mills in the background, Milford Haven, c. 1905.

Castle Pill waterway, Milford Haven, 1913.

The Scotch Bay shipbreakers' yard, Milford Haven, 1919.

The new Victoria Bridge was opened on 12 October 1933 at a final building cost of £45,000.
Eight steamrollers are pictured here trundling across the bridge to convince the public of the
new construction's strength.

The famous Marloes village clock, 1906. It was erected in 1904 as a memorial to the 4th Baron Kensington who owned twelve square miles of land in the locality.

The village stores and Marloes post office (the postmaster at this time was a Mr Edwards), Milford Haven, 1910. The village's water pump can be seen on the left.

Four

Neyland and Llangwn

Honeyborough Village Green, Neyland, 1904.

Locals pose for the photographer in the High Street, Neyland, 1903.

Cambrian House and Biddlecombe's shop which advertised as the 'House for Best Value in Drapery', High Street, Neyland, 1905.

Great Eastern Terrace, c. 1904. The street was named to commemorate the visit of the *SS Great Eastern* at Neyland in August 1860.

A dray delivering the morning milk in Picton Road, Neyland, 1906.

Hazelbeach, Neyland, 1912.

A dredging ship anchored on the foreshore at Hazelbeach, Neyland, c. 1910.

Mastlebridge, Neyland, 1912.

The hamlet of Neyland Vale, 1915.

GWR steam train approaching Westfield Crossing, Neyland, 1920.

South Wales Hotel, Neyland, 1909.

GWR approach road with the South Wales Hotel in the background, Neyland, 1912.

South Wales Hotel,
Neyland.

The imposing South Wales Hotel, Neyland, c. 1919. At the bus stop two of Green's buses stop en route to Haverfordwest and Milford Haven.

Brunel's Neyland in its heyday with the busy GWR train terminus, goods marshalling yards and floating pontoon, 1913.

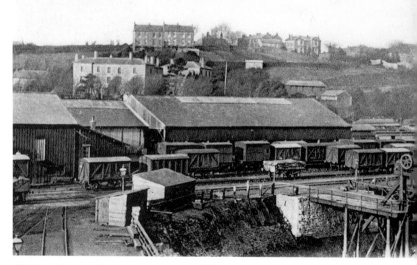

GWR goods marshalling yard at Neyland in 1909.

Barnlake, Neyland, 1930.

Official opening of the Neyland Ice Factory by Lady Phillips on 16 November 1908. Photograph by Sam Allen.

The Neyland Ice Factory, 1910.

Barnlake ferry and the fish landing stage, Neyland, 1906.

Neyland fishmarket workers in 1913. The market closed the following year.

The fish landing stage and a general view of Neyland, 1908.

Villagers pose for the camera in Llangwm's Main Street, 1906.

Llangwm children in the Main Street, 1906.

Main Street, Llangwm, c. 1917 showing the business of Mr J. Thomas, family butcher on the right.

The Llangwm foreshore, c. 1908. From left to right: Elsie Morgans, Olwen Morgans, Sylvia Morgans, grandmother Mrs Betty Morgans. The man with the child is Mr Billy Davies.

The famous market boat which assisted the legendary Llangwm fisherwomen in crossing the Haven. Fresh catches of fish, cockles, mussels, shrimps, prawns and oysters would be carried in willow panniers and baskets. The areas visited by the women included Pembroke, Stackpole, Tenby, Narberth and Carmarthen.

*Left:*Llangwm's celebrated fisherwoman, Dolly Palmer dressed in her distinctive clothing and carrying a shoulder pannier and basket of fish, 1904. Photograph by Sam Allen. *Right:*Llangwm fisherwomen at Tenby's Goscar Rock with the harbour in the background, 1905.

Five

Pembroke (*Penfro*) and Pembroke Dock (*Doc Penfro*)

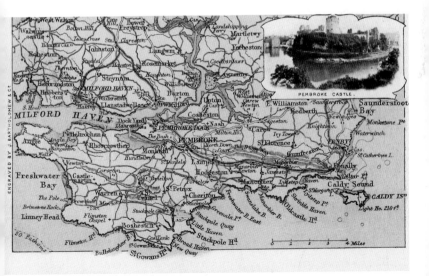

John Walker's map postcard advertising Pembroke Castle, 1908.

Pembroke Castle, once the central strategic fortress of the 'Little England beyond Wales'. It was the birthplace of the first Tudor monarch, Henry VII.

Main Street, Pembroke, 1904.

Bush Street, Pembroke Dock, c. 1910.

Queen Street and Diamond Street, Pembroke Dock, c. 1910.

Above: Panoramic view over Pembroke Dock from the Barrack Hill, c. 1907. The ship building hangers are clearly visible along the shoreline.

Left: The Centenary Monument (1814-1914) with its domed lights was built in Albion Square and unveiled on 15 July 1914. It was erected by public subscription to commemorate the centenary of the building of Pembroke Dock and its Royal Dockyard.

Victoria Road with, in the background, the dockyard to the left and Hobbs Point on the right, c. 1905.

The stone-built defensible barracks and drawbridge, Pembroke Dock, c. 1915.

The last Sunderland flying boat ML 824 at the Pembroke Dock airbase. The RAF established a flying boat base here in 1930 and it remained open for almost thirty years.

The *Cleddau King* succeeded the *Cleddau Queen* as the Neyland to Pembroke Dock ferryboat.

Military Road leading to the Royal Engineers barracks, Pennar, Pembroke Dock, c. 1915.

Embellished bill dated September 1893 from J. McMaster & Co., timber and slate merchants, Pembroke Dock.

A two-part programme image on the left:

A Procession

Will be formed at the
MARKET HALL,
At 5.30 p.m., on
WEDNESDAY, April 2nd, 1919
OF OUR HEROES & GALLANT
SONS,
Led by . .
THE POLICE, HIS WORSHIP THE
MAYOR (J. GIBBY, ESQ.), COUN-
CILLORS AND COMMITTEE, and
headed by the . .

Town Band,

Will proceed via
Commercial Row,
Queen Street,
Dimond Street,
Gwyther Street,
Bush Street, &
Albion Square
And return to the Market
Hall,
Where the Troops will be
entertained to HIGH TEA,
assembled at the tables.
Friends of the Men will be ad-
mitted to the Hall by the North
Door at 6-15—6.30 p.m.

Market Hall,

FINIS CORONAT OPUS
1914 ★ 1919

PEMBROKE-DOCK

Welcome

Home

AND - -

Presentation of

Souvenirs

To its Gallant Boys,

**Wednesday, April 2nd,
1919.**

J. THOMAS, TYP.

Left: Programme for the welcome home celebrations for the 'gallant boys' from Pembroke Dock who had served King and country during the First World War, 2 April 1919.

Opposite above: Invitation from Pembroke Dock Police to celebrate the termination of First World War hostilities, 1919.

Programme

FOR THE

**FIRST SECTION OF
OUR BOYS
WELCOMED HOME**

Preparatory to serving High Tea
6.15 p.m., Grace
will be offered by the Vicar, Rev. D. L.
Prosser, M.A.

High Tea.

Selections by the Band.

7 p.m., Thanksgiving
by the Rev. J. Griffiths (Albion Square)

Interval 7.15 to 7.45 p.m.

8 p.m., HIS WORSHIP THE MAYOR
(J. GIBBY, Esq.), & MEMBERS OF THE
CORPORATION,

Will confer the Honorary
Freedom of the Borough

ON

C. S. M. ARGYLE, R.E., D.C.M. &
Belgian Croix de Guerre.
Q. M. S. WILCOX, B.G.A., Belgian
Croix de Guerre.
SERGT. MACDONALD, Welsh Gds.,
D.C.M.
PTE. J. REES, R.W.F., M.M.
And also decorate
SERGT. A. GWYTHER, 4th Welsh,
with the honoured distinction of .
the Military Medal. . . . . .
To be followed by a . . . .

8.30 p.m.

Smoking Concert
and the **Presentation
of Diplomas of Honour.**

OVERTURE by the TOWN BAND,
(Under the conductorship of Mr. T. James,
Bandmaster)
Toast (1) The King—His Worship the Mayor
Musical Honours.
Song ... ... The Dear Homeland
Miss Alicia Cove, L.R.A.M.
Toast (2) Our Guests—Councillr W. Smith
Recitation ... The ex-Burglar's Story
Mr. Thomas, A.L.C.M.
**FIRST PRESENTATION OF DIPLOMAS
OF HONOUR**
By His Worship the Mayor & Mayoress.
Musical Honours.
Song ... ... The Glory of the Sea.
Miss Alicia Cove.
Response to Toast 2.
Mr. W. B. MORSE (Navy)
Mr. E. J. WAKEY (Army)
Monologue ... ... Devil may Care
Mr. Thomas
2nd PRESENTATION OF DIPLOMAS,
(as above)
Song ... ... A Short Cut
Miss Alicia Cove
Recitation ... British Workman's Rights
Mr. Thomas.
3rd PRESENTATION OF DIPLOMAS,
(as above)
Burlesque Duett ... Keys of Heaven
Miss Alicia Cove & Mr. Thomas
Selection by the Band | National Anthem
Accompanist - Miss Powell, A.L.C.M.

Right: The order of events for the 1919 celebrations.

Opposite below: Bill from Bowling Brothers of Pembroke Dock dated 1 July 1892.

Pembroke Dock Police "Peace" Outing

29th JUNE, 1919.

The pleasure of your company is requested to visit FRESHWATER WEST, near Angle, on above date, for the purpose of all Police Officers, their Wives & Families, joining to celebrate the termination of Hostilities.

Conveyances will leave "Pensarn" at 8 a.m.

Refreshments, etc., provided.

W. GEO. THOMAS, Supt.

By kind permission of F. T. B. SUMMERS, Esq.,
Chief Constable of Pembrokeshire.

44,
DIMOND-ST,
Pem-Dock

BOWLING BROTHERS

AND
AUCTION MART
Commercial
Row.

(Auctioneers to the Lords' Commissioners of the Admiralty)

GENERAL AUCTIONEERS, VALUERS,

House Insurance, and Commission Agents

Mr W. G. Griffiths, Market St, Tenby

BOUGHT at ...... Bristol Haze Sale March 1 1892

Payable to J. H. BOWLING, 44, Dimond-St., or T. G. BOWLING, 18, Commercial Row,

Pembroke-Dock, or their order on the 1st day of July 1892 See below.

Fol. 93

All amounts under Five Shillings are due at the time of Sale. Jany 28.93

Lot		£	s	d
	Spring Mattras & Interest	1	1	2

Feby 1 1893 Received with thanks

Pembroke Dock division of the Pembrokeshire Police, 1919.

Six

Saundersfoot and Tenby
(*Dinbych–y–Pysgod*)

Gardening staff at the Swallow Tree Gardens during the First World War.

Saundersfoot Boy Scouts.

Above: Saundersfoot Boy Scouts, 1916. From right to left, back row: Lawson Frost, Ronnie Griffiths, Reggie Frost, Cyril Day, Revd Randell (Curate at St Issell's), Harold Thomas, Tom Griffiths, William Hewitt, Fred Phillips. Middle row: Eddie Phillips, Albert Howells, Jack Jones, Stanley Ormond, Tom Parry, Lloyd Frost, Lewis Craig. Front row: Hughie Griffiths, Edgar Davies, Jack Beynon, Ivor Davies, Willie Williams.

Mr Albert Howells, pictured above in the middle row, has had a distinguished career since being a boy scout. This son of the village went first to Llanelli to start his apprenticeship in the pharmaceutical industry. It was the beginning of a long and celebrated career which resulted in him visiting many Commonwealth countries in the conduct of his work. In 1968 he became the President of the Pharmaceutical Society of Great Britain and in 1970 he was awarded the OBE for his tremendous contribution to pharmacy. He is also a Freeman of the City of London and in 1979 he received the Charter Gold Medal of the Pharmaceutical Society of Great Britain. He has led a full and active life as the pharmacy ambassador of Britain and though not in good health he still reminisces fondly about Saundersfoot's past.

Opposite: Three generations of the Morgan family have been associated with the sea: Mr Wilfred Morgan (seen at the wheel), his son, Mr Cedric Morgan (current Harbour Master), and his grandson, Mr Andy Morgan. This portrait was taken in 1960.

America seems to have been the theme in this 1920s entry in the Saundersfoot Carnival. From left to right: Eddie Phillips, Lawson Frost, Leslie Griffiths, Willie Frost, Ivy Baldwin, Marjorie Howells.

Cart at the top of the Glen delivering water to houses not on the main supply, 1934. Sunny Bank bungalow is in the background.

Right: Unveiling the War Memorial at Saundersfoot, 11 November 1923 - 'to the lasting honour of the men of St Issell's parish who died in the Great War 1914-1918'.

Below: The canvas sails of the coal schooners dry in the wind, Saundersfoot harbour, c. 1870. The coal loading chute can be seen on the left. Photograph by Mortimer Allen.

Pupils at Saundersfoot Council School in 1921. *Above:* the infants class; note the toy bear in the centre of the picture. *Below:* children from standards 1 and 2.

A.R. Quinton's *Tenby and Caldey Island*, 1930. Alfred Robert Quinton was probably the best known of all postcard artists. He specialized in water colour drawings of town and country views and was particularly successful in reflecting the character of rural life. This, and the other Tenby scenes below, were printed and published by J. Salmon in the early 1930s.

Tenby from the Slopes.

The North Sands, Tenby.

Tenby Harbour.

Above: Tenby Pier and Bay.

Right: Ancient Walls and Church, Tenby painted by
Frank Lewis Emanuel in 1903. Emanuel came
to Tenby to paint in oils in the early 1900s.
Each of his fifteen paintings of Tenby were later
produced as postcards by Raphael Tuck. Most of
these cards reveal the artist's name in one
of the corners.

WARREN STREET, Tenby *Nov 9th* **189** 2

Mr Griffiths *Fish Merchant*

BOUGHT OF

The Tenby & Pembroke Cycle Compy.,

Manager: GEORGE ACE, Cycling Champion of Wales, 1879 to 1889, (retired)

Cycle Manufacturers & Wholesale Factors

OF MUSICAL INSTRUMENTS OF EVERY DESCRIPTION, SUSPENSION PERAMBULATORS, MAIL CARTS, WASHERS, MANGLES, WRINGERS, SEWING MACHINES, TENNIS, GOLF, CRICKET, BILLIARD, BAGATELLE, WATERPROOFS FOR FISHING, AND ALL SPORTING REQUISITES.

ANY ARTICLE SUPPLIED ON THE HIRE PURCHASE SYSTEM

TERMS................ Telegrams: "ACE, TENBY."

Cigar and Cigarette Importers.

Fancy Warehousemen.

Agent for JAS. PAIN & SON'S FIREWORKS.

Wheeler & Wilson's Genuine Sewing Machines

1892

Nov 4th Four Dozen Regulation Trawlers Red Flares 5/3 13 -

Bill, dated 9 November 1892, from the Tenby and Pembroke Cycle Company.

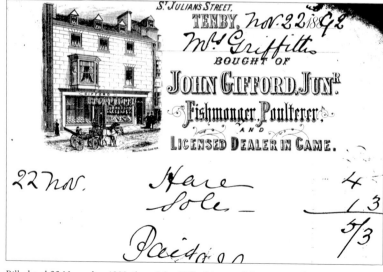

ST JULIANS STREET,

TENBY, *Nov 22* 18 92

Mrs Griffiths

BOUGHT OF

JOHN GIFFORD, JUNR.

Fishmonger, Poulterer,

AND

LICENSED DEALER IN GAME.

22 Nov. Hare 4

Sole — 1 3

5/3

Paidson

Bill, dated 22 November 1892, from John Gifford Junior, fishmonger and poulterer, Tenby.

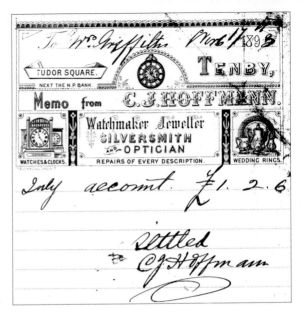

To Wⁿ Griffiths Nov 17 1893

TUDOR SQUARE.
NEXT THE N.P. BANK.

TENBY,

Memo from C. J. HOFFMANN.

Watchmaker Jeweller
SILVERSMITH AND **OPTICIAN**

WATCHES & CLOCKS.   REPAIRS OF EVERY DESCRIPTION.   WEDDING RINGS.

2nly account £1. 2. 6

Settled
CJ Hoffman

Bill, dated 17 November 1893 from C.J. Hoffmann, Tenby watchmaker and jeweller.

1, CAMPBELL HOUSE,
HIGH STREET, TENBY,
189 3

Mrs Griffiths

To H. MORTIMER ALLEN,
Portrait and Landscape Photographer.
Fine Art and Fancy Dealer.
PICTURES OF EVERY DESCRIPTION FRAMED AT LOWEST PRICES.

1892			
Dec 3	6 Photos " (Baby)	6"	–
23	1 Xmas Card	2"	–
	1 " " "	1"	6
24	" " "		9
		10"	3

Paid
H. M. Allen
Feb 16" 1893

Bill from H. Mortimer Allen, the Tenby photographer.

91

Tudor Square. **Tenby.** *Xmas* 1893

Next Door to Post Office.

212

Mr W. Griffiths

TO JOHN EVANS,

Saddle & Harness

MANUFACTURER.

BOOT & SHOE WAREHOUSEMAN.

BOOTS & SHOES OF EVERY DESCRIPTION
IN STOCK & MADE TO ORDER.

5 PER CENT CHARGED ON ALL OVERDUE A/CS.

FOR MANTEAUS TRUNKS
& TRAVELLING REQUISITES.

TERMS HALY YEARLY A/CS.

AN ASSORTMENT
OF LADIES' & GENTLEMEN'S
WATERPROOFS IN STOCK
& MADE TO MEASURE.

TERMS. QUARTERLY A/CS.

1893   Saddlery a/c

Aug 5th   New Leather to Vessel Pump   *£   1   6*

Bill from John Evans, saddle and harness manufacturer, Tenby, Christmas 1893.

Tenby Rangers, photographed at the Scout and Guide Headquarters in Warren Street, Tenby, 1926. Among those pictured are the District Commissioner, Maud Pudsey Dawson; Inez Kingdom; Virginia Copland; Blodwen Griffiths: Maisie Beddoe.

Seven

Narberth (*Arberth*) and Clunderwen

Local children pose for the photographer on the Square in Narberth, 1914.

Plain Dealings Road, Narberth, c. 1906.

High Street, Narberth, 1913.

Large crowds attend the horse and Castlemartin Black cattle sales in the High Street, Narberth, c. 1904.

John Brothers Grocery and General Stores, Compton House, No 8 High Street, Narberth, 1912.

The Cross Lane pig fair, Narberth, 1904.

St James' Street, Narberth, 1914. Photograph by Mortimer Allen.

Market day in the Market Square, Narberth, 1912.

The Court House and the premises of W. Burgess, printer and stationer, Narberth, c. 1908.

The Intermediate School, Narberth with the entrance for girls on the right and for boys on the left, 1911. Photograph by Willie John.

Station Road, Narberth, 1912.

Narberth railway station, c. 1907. After completion of the 273 yard Blackaldern Tunnel in August 1866, Narberth station was officially opened the following month.

Narberth Harlequins Football Club, 1908. Photograph by Willie John.

Clunderwen village, c. 1913.

High Street, Clunderwen, 1911. Photograph by Willie John.

Right: The Clunderwen Farmers Co-operative Association's building pictured after the disastrous fire of 18 October 1922. Photograph by Willie John.

Below: The old custom of holding a rope across the road to impede the passage of a newly-married couple, High Street, Clunderwen, 1909. Photograph by Willie John.

Mr Elias Jenkins was always associated with The Emporium, High Street, Clunderwen up until 1906. Afterwards the premises came under new management.

Eight

Other Pembrokeshire Villages

Main Road, Johnston, c. 1905. St Peter's Church is on the right.

The village of Houghton, c. 1912. Photograph by David Bowen.

The seaside village of Broad Haven, c. 1906. It has also been referred to as 'Broad Heaven' because of the restful atmosphere to be found here.

Stalls are assembled in readiness for the annual Little Haven hiring fair, c. 1907. This was always held on 1 November - All Saints' Day.

Strawberry Road and the Point, Little Haven, 1920.

The funeral of Lord Cawdor, Mr F.A.V. Campbell at Cheriton Church, Pembroke, with the Bluejackets leading the bier to the church, February 1911.

Cosheston village, 1912. Photograph by Sam Allen.

Cresselly House, c. 1912. Photograph by Mortimer Allen.

The village of Manorbier, c. 1912.

David Lloyd George, then Chancellor of the Exchequer, presenting medals to the Pembrokeshire Yeomanry at Penally Camp in 1912. Photograph by Mortimer Allen.

Penally village and railway station with St Nicholas' Church in the background, c. 1906.

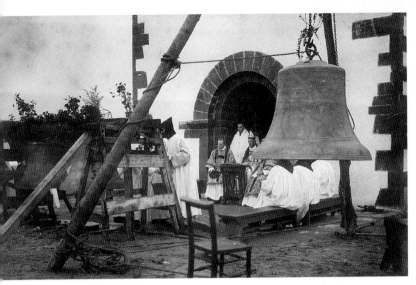

Blessing the monastery bells on the island of Caldey, c. 1912. In May 1931 the bells were removed and taken to Prinknash.

The Four Cross, Begelly

The Four Cross Roads, Begelly. Note the RAC roadside box alongside the road leading away to the right, 1932.

The Railway Inn, Kilgetty, 1928.

Kilgetty GWR road bridge advertising the Royal Gatehouse Hotel in Tenby - 'The Motorist's Mecca', 1938. Merriman the ironmonger's can be seen in the forground to the right while beyond the bridge were Bridge Stores - the business of Mr George Edwards; the Co-operative Society and Hooper's Motor Garage.

The village of Stepaside, near Kilgetty, with its ironworks and the Grove Colliery, 1924.
Stepaside Fair can be seen in the centre foreground.

Stepaside post office, 1914. Photograph by Mortimer Allen.

The coastal village of Amroth, c. 1907. Over the years rough seas have eroded and undermined many properties. In 1931, for example, severe storms caused serious damage to the front cottages and gardens. Photograph by Sam Allen.

Amroth carnival and sports day, 1908. Photograph by Sam Allen

Templeton GWR station, c. 1910. The new and larger signal box on the 'up' railway line was opened on 1 May 1906. With the closure of the Templeton brickworks in the 1920s the local economy and employment levels were greatly affected. Photograph by Sam Allen.

The productive Gelly Woollen Mills, Clunderwen, c. 1904. The building was destroyed by fire on 14 January 1938. Photograph by Sam Allen.

Clarbeston Road post office, 1936.

Clarbeston Road GWR junction, 1908.

Blacksmith's shop on the village green, Spittal, 1937.

Commercial Hotel, Ford, Wolf's Castle, 1907.

Pentre Garage and Lloyds Bank on The Square, Letterston, 1935.

Mrs Jenkins stands in the doorway of her Letterston shop, c. 1906.

The general stores and post office of Mr William Rees situated near the route of the cattle drovers, Puncheston, 1905.

The village of New Moat, c. 1926.

Castle Hotel and the village stores, Maenclochog, c. 1910. Photograph by Willie John.

Hen Capel and Picton House situated near the village green, Maenclochog, c. 1929.

Ponthywel Bridge near Maenclochog, c. 1907. Photograph by Willie John.

Railway staff and associates photographed on the platform of 'Y Lein Fach', Rosebush station, c. 1906. Photograph from the Gwyn Briwnant Jones collection.

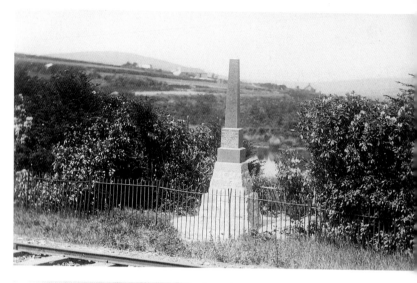

CORONATION BONFIRE AT ROSEBUSH

Above: The Railway Monument at Rosebush, 1913.
Photograph by Willie John.

Left: Bonfire erected and lit at Rosebush to
celebrate the coronation of King George V in
1911. Photograph by Willie John.

The footbridge, Mynachlogddu, c. 1912.

BRYNBERIAN

Singing festival at Brynberian, c. 1928. Note Mynydd Preseli in the background. Photograph by Charles Edwards.

The main street in Crymmych, c. 1908.

The annual Crymmych Fair, which is held on the last Tuesday in August, c. 1912.

Dale village, 1910.

Boncath Inn and the village stores, c. 1912.

Newgale village, 1920.

The quay at Solva, an important early trading port for the local community, c. 1904.

Right: Trelerwr Cottage Church near St David's. It was occupied by Robert Frood (seated on the left) and his wife, Martha seen knitting in the doorway, c. 1904.

Below: The Cross Square, St David's, c. 1906.

The Greek ship *Emmanuel* which was driven onto the rocks in Ramsey Sound, March 1925.

A workman surveys the damaged hull of the *Emmanuel* in the dry dock, Milford Haven, April 1925.

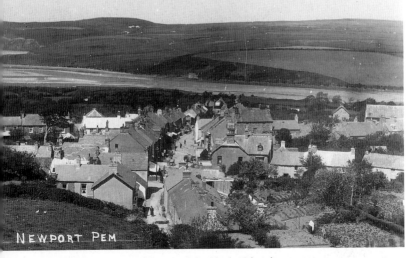

The village of Newport, c. 1928. Photograph by Charles Edwards.

St Davids City Green Granite Drinking Fountain May 1912.

Left: The green granite drinking fountain in The Square, St David's, May 1912.

Below: The windmill, St David's, 1906. It was later converted to the Twr-y-felin Hotel.

THE WINDMILL, St DAVIDS, CONVERTED TO TWR-Y-FELIN HOTEL 1906. JT.